# The Early Days of This

*poems by*

# Jacqueline Sullivan

*Finishing Line Press*
Georgetown, Kentucky

# The Early Days of This

Copyright © 2022 by Jacqueline Sullivan
ISBN 978-1-64662-996-1 First Edition
All rights reserved under International and Pan-American Copyright Conventions. No part of this book may be reproduced in any manner whatsoever without written permission from the publisher, except in the case of brief quotations embodied in critical articles and reviews.

## ACKNOWLEDGMENTS

I gratefully acknowledge the following publications in which these poems first appeared:

"What Poetry Is"—originally published in *The Maine Review*, Volume 4, Number 2
"Sonnet for a Neighbor's Lilies"—originally published in *Common Ground Review*, Volume 21, Number 1
"Translating the *Aeneid*"—originally published in *Slant*, Volume XXXI, 2017

My thanks also to everyone in the Workshop for Publishing Poets, its founder, Barbara Helfgott-Hyett, and to all of my teachers.

I offer my deepest gratitude to my family and to those ancestors who came before who I'm certain had a hand in these poems.

Publisher: Leah Huete de Maines
Editor: Christen Kincaid
Cover Art: Jacqueline Sullivan
Author Photo: Jacqueline Sullivan
Cover Design: Elizabeth Maines McCleavy

Order online: www.finishinglinepress.com
        also available on amazon.com

Author inquiries and mail orders:
Finishing Line Press
PO Box 1626
Georgetown, Kentucky 40324
USA

# Table of Contents

Sonnet for a Neighbor's Lilies ............... 1

Only a Few Seasons ............... 2

Pesellino's *Virgin and Child with a Swallow* ............... 3

What Poetry Is ............... 4

A Red Geranium ............... 5

News Break ............... 6

Nightingale ............... 7

The Queen's Speech ............... 8

Ticker Tape under Task Force Briefing ............... 9

Keeping Up ............... 10

Notre-Dame, One Year Later ............... 11

Perspective ............... 12

Picture Window ............... 13

Poem, in Place Of ............... 14

Flipping through the Dictionary ............... 15

My Nephew with Long Hair ............... 16

Translating the *Aeneid* ............... 17

Reading Pushkin in Winter ............... 18

How to Paint a Rose ............... 19

*In loving memory of my parents*

*Beauty is truth, truth beauty,—that is all
Ye know on earth, and all ye need to know.*
　　　　　　*—John Keats*

**Sonnet for a Neighbor's Lilies**

The empty bin spells demolition, spring's rusty beginning,
holds remnants of what they left or couldn't take—collections:
lamps, umbrellas, things wept on, even a GE microwave.
Now men descend in hard hats at seven a.m.

One hard-shoulders the back door which refuses to yield.
The rest push against a window unaware
beneath their boots bloomed lilies of the field.
Inside they do what they need to, make the roof disappear.

All that's left is a somber lot,
a backhoe, and a pickup truck
with Someone & Sons scrawled across the side.
Even the view of the pond someday may be gone.

But the forsythia lining the edge with raggedy tendrils
continue to burst through, bright yellow.

**Only a Few Seasons**

My sister phones me for advice
about ordering tulip bulbs.

Rattles off color choices
either in Latin or floral species talk.
I translate silently in my head,
tell her Angelique and Black Parrot
make a good match, mostly
based on the names.

She warns me they won't last,
no matter how great the year before.
You can only squeeze out a few seasons.
I thought they'd keep coming up forever—
once buried they could be trusted
to repeat their Daliesque beauty.

I have expected too much
of April.

### Pesellino's *Virgin and Child with a Swallow*

The child holds a swallow
looks out into the distance
knows what the future holds
knows even at his tender age
a war can break out at any time.

The swallow must be the world
and all of us, small things
in need of repair.
After all, we can only do so much
with our light feathers and wings.

He clutches that swallow
a bit too tight
the way children do
the way they hold on
and won't let go.

It's been said that swallows
catch the souls of the dead
which must be why sailors
tattoo them on their arms
in case of drowning.

The Virgin holds her child
knows she can't keep him
safe on her lap forever
like any mother knows
she has to let go.

Pesellino, himself, gone
by the time he was thirty-five.
He must have known
a great deal
about swallows.

## What Poetry Is

My brother phoned to say he'd seen six robins in his pine tree
like those we used to see outside our grandmother's kitchen
where we'd watch her make baking powder biscuits
on Sundays, cast iron frying pan in hand as robins sang.
She'd barely touch the dough, let it take shape and wait
for it to rise as robins rose in branches of uncluttered sky.
When the oil began to smoke, she'd drop in each pale globe,
little ships bumping about on a black sea,
they'd turn color and puff, curved and amber-chested.
When ready, she'd place on yellow-flowered plates to please us,
her white-blond hair a mystery to children who knew nothing of
Norse invaders and cholera or how she got here
in her blue check dress as tall as a ship, those blue checks
like bright blue eggs a robin lays uncamouflaged and unafraid
within a twig-brown nest.

**A Red Geranium**

The gravestone holds their initials, witness
to his quiet grief only his dates incomplete.
A cobbled road back home
lay between them on first meeting,
hardly as wide as this space,
he gestures to a gentle infantry
in its place.

He kneels before the broken air,
before everything antique and fair –
scattered hillsides, relentless daffodils in prayer.
Her voice was a red geranium, all he ever needed.
The ground between them now is soft and airy.
The workers have made rows of holes in it
for spring.

## News Break

From inside I watch my neighbor plant a tree
as dusk turns into a blanket of gray cobwebs
making it harder and harder to see.
Its simple leaves are shades of hazelnut
in the dying sun spiraling into autumn.
He struggles with the heavy root ball,
Sisyphus to this burlap captive,
tug and pull, drag and push until
it's too dark to see if he's succeeded.
The next day it looks a bit crooked
in the sober light of morning.
I want to go and fix it
but relent knowing soon
the sun will straighten it.

**Nightingale**

Retrieving a Band-Aid from the medicine chest
I gaze in the mirror, realize I've lost
track of days during the pandemic.
I put it over the sliver-crack in my finger,
hope for a real fix for what we've been plastered with—
therapeutics, a vaccine, even the intercession of
St. Benedict and I recall the small white index cards
from the pediatrician on Brattle Street
my mother kept for each of us,
full names and dates of birth at the top
in her immaculate penmanship as if we
were England's future kings and queens.
Next, a list of potential diseases:
Tuberculosis, Mumps, Measles,
Rubella, Small Pox, Polio, et alia,
a precise inoculation date beside each.
As it turned out the only thing that stole
our youth was in the dust of passing summers.
She ordered our days, our own Nightingale,
softly admonishing patience was a virtue.

**The Queen's Speech**

The Queen appears in an emerald dress
assures us we'll meet again in the perfect shade
of lipstick. It's been said she has one thousand
different varieties of roses outside her palace
where reams of garden-keepers tend them as if
they were their own tucked in luxurious beds.
There's even an outlandish Napoleonic vase, spoils
of another war, but those roses are without a care,
kitchen-garlic keeps away the pests and for the final act
ladybugs come in and make a curtain call of munching.

This afternoon I'll go into my yard, collect the fallen willow
shards as weak as wilted daisies from last night's storm.

**Ticker Tape under Task Force Briefing**

Italy reopens book, stationary, and baby clothes stores.
I didn't hear about la drogheria, too peppered with news
about numbers of the dead, notices posted
in bold-black letters on wooden church doors
for the offering up of prayers. After all this
perhaps it's time for a pen and hand-lettered condolences,
engaging in an epistolary way, not some lifeless
email buried in the tomb of a spam folder.

I wonder about my relatives in San Leonardo surrounded
by sea, hopefully hemming them in like a massive spleen.
How we drove at breakneck speed in that tiny black fiat
whirling through the concrete roundabout we hardly took
notice of the statue to the dead in the center while back home
loaves of handmade bread waited for us like the last supper.

**Keeping Up**

A little boy learns
to ride a cobalt bike
at dusk when no one's out
only his Dad trailing him
at a safe distance
out of breath but keeping up
jogging behind in Adidas kicks
that haven't been out
in years.

**Notre-Dame, One Year Later**

Irresistible shell of your former self
backbone of the 4th arrondissement
you're temporarily hunched in shadow.
We had a massive unintended falling out.
I miss your certain features, semi-decimated,
your Gothic architecture now a cage of evidence
and the humble rows of straw-seated chairs
dedicated to Our Lady are filled instead
with lavender that's lost its way.
Yet despite these mysteries
and sorrows your rose windows
still accept chandeliers of daily grace.

Last Wednesday your great bell again rang out
as all of Paris gathered on balconies, clapping.

**Perspective**

Tints of frost on rooftops
glitter like light soaked interiors
as I climb to the top of Robbins Hill
the city in pewter distance.

Parsley-like buds on foreground trees
commence their display of leaves,
provide a cushion for the eye
in morning's coronation.

In the early days of this, I found
and dusted off a framed Bonnard print
from the Tate Gallery where we went
in and out one carefree summer.

His pen and ink pot still sit silently,
untouched, near paper and a few maroon
and mauve-covered books
on a table overlooking Paris.

**Picture Window**

Forced to reflect on nature like Keats or Shelley
except from inside kitchens, dens, and living rooms,
it's a good time to bring Jane Austen into view,
she, who compared men to rocks and mountains
must have had a serious pandemic of
broken hearts to come up with that one.

Among many "desk-breaks" I've become familiar
with a reappearing bluebird I call Daedalus
last seen a few days ago (or has it been a week).
He was responsible for a minor misdemeanor
not an exciting crime nevertheless he tangled with
a white napkin or perhaps a page from someone's journal.

It finally got the best of him and he succumbed
dropped it where the shock of wind forced it against a fence.
Oh Daedalus, what have you brought—forgotten rites of spring,
an accounting of the passage of time, or a sketch of a newly
bought prom dress with lilac crinoline, never worn,
minor detritus from a certain time of plague.

**Poem, in Place Of**
*in mem. M.J.B.*

We would have filed in greeted by the scent of lilies
tiny cards attached to stems so far
away it would be hard to see who sent them.

The family in a row as straight as soldiers would wait
for our approach and in your hands for company
a ruby-colored rosary.

How you used to run full steam
behind the celery-colored station wagon
squinting into angles of softly falling sun.

Yesterday's a door half-open
a piece of your profile in light
above a polished necktie.

For a final blessing,
you deserve a poem by Tennyson.

## Flipping through the Dictionary

I look at a black & white photo
labeled "Woman with Dudeen"
and wonder how lucky it might be
to end up such a mythology
ancient and staring ahead
as smoke curls from a pipe of clay
which looks as if it could have been
at a centuries earlier Druid fest
where they would have planned
to scatter and outlast even weather.
Maybe tonight I'll dream of
my mother, her jet-black hair
which at some point she let go
as white as marble.

## My Nephew with Long Hair

pushed a lawnmower through ankle high grass
leaving clippings behind,
the way a child leaves psalms,
leaves faded t-shirts, shyness.
His thick black curls barely managed
by a scarlet leather headband
stolen from his sister's bureau.
Sometimes he'd brandish a topknot
for a graduation or christening
then he let his tendrils fall
onto what became a forest floor
thick with moss and shadow.

He could have been micro-tiled in Rome
during the reign of Constantine
as decorated as a fourth-century warrior,
a Gothic Chieftain with feathers in his braids,
or living in a Gaelic hill fort
always ready with a blade
who left rings of stone behind him.
Pick a dynasty, he did the hair
then out of the blue
he cut it all off,
went away,
left the eternal.

## Translating the *Aeneid*

Latin IV with Mr. Murray,
twelve of us, a jury of the past,
teenagers on the way
to hexameter translation.
Virgil's *Aeneid*, Epic of Rome,
our antique destination.
We sit in alphabetical order,
known by last names only,
Doherty, Gallagher, Russo, et alia.
We don't make a move without Aeneas,
our hero, in Classroom Three.
*Sunt lacrimae rerum et mentem mortalia tangunt.*
(There are tears for things and mortal things touch the mind.)

We begin with what we already know,
there are tears and we are here.
In the margins, youthful scribbles:
pet stag (a favorite); simile (used excessively);
prophecy (exotic); and chariot (of the past).
That about covers it.
Streams pass quickly over rocks.
Aeneas has only seven ships left
and we haven't even finished Book One.
Sometimes it's the most basic lesson:
you will have a limited number of ships,
you will eventually lose most if not all of them,
learn to keep sailing.

## Reading Pushkin in Winter

A major winter snowstorm
is forecast for tomorrow
and I'll be reading Pushkin's
*A Magic Moment I Remember*
better than a confection.
How time passed. How before
time passed everything was
a beginning. The falling snow
already a mile high
soon will be forgotten.
I hope the weathermen
are wrong, think ahead
to spring then back
to that last summer.
I can't even see the pair
of Adirondack chairs
in the backyard where
we used to sit listening
to the Counting Crows
*A Long December* spilling
from your transistor radio,
yesterday's newspaper
folded neatly nearby,
already read.

## How to Paint a Rose

It may seem mundane watching a man paint a rose on TV but don't turn away, watch as he works on the first few petals, back and forth, palette to paper, making some darker, others lighter, then darker again almost cancelling out the rose. He says when looking at a rose figure out which side is in shade, which reflects light, keep adding and mixing until right, like the Permanent Rose of my mother's lipstick, the shade she wore whenever she left the house, her silver-buttoned car coat crackling as the steering wheel caught each round button or the way sunset catches billboards in southern California, flashing Vermillion in the rear view. When the rose begins to look real, he trims each petal in Titanium White, adds a sparrow, tiny and dark, above its large knob so even if no one is watching there will still be a witness. It's not as if I have any plans to paint a rose but I keep watching so if in the future I had the chance to do something beautiful I might know how.

Jacqueline Sullivan's poems have appeared in numerous journals including *Cold Mountain Review, The Briar Cliff Review, Slant, The Maine Review,* and *Common Ground Review.* She is an attorney and has also been a Joshua A. Guberman Teaching Fellow and Lecturer at Brandeis University, a lecturer at Northeastern University, and a lecturer at Boston University School of Law. This is her first chapbook.

www.ingramcontent.com/pod-product-compliance
Lightning Source LLC
LaVergne TN
LVHW041524070426
835507LV00012B/1806